POLICE CARS

by Jill Braithwaite

Pull Ahead Books

Lerner Publications Company • Minneapolis

W

Special thanks to Officer Amy Springer of the Savage, Minnesota, Police Department.

Copyright © 2004 by Lerner Publications Company

This book is available in two editions:
Library binding by Lerner Publications Company, a division of Lerner Publishing Group
Soft cover by First Avenue Editions, an imprint of Lerner Publishing Group
241 First Avenue North
Minneapolis, MN 55401 U.S.A.

Website address: www.lernerbooks.com

Library of Congress Cataloging-in-Publication Data

Braithwaite, Jill.
    Police cars / by Jill Braithwaite.
        p.   cm. – (Pull ahead books)
    Includes index.
    Summary: An introduction to the features and uses of
police cars.
        ISBN: 0–8225–0770–6 (lib. bdg. : alk. paper)
        ISBN: 0–8225–9919–8 (pbk. : alk. paper)
        1. Police vehicles–Juvenile literature. [1. Police
vehicles.] I. Title. II. Series.
    HV7936.V4B73 2004
    363.2'32–dc22   2003019391

Manufactured in the United States of America
1 2 3 4 5 6 – JR – 09 08 07 06 05 04

Vroom! Zoom! A police car speeds by.

Lights flash
and sirens
wail. They
warn drivers
to get out of
the way.

Police cars help police officers do their work. They get police officers where they are needed fast.

Powerful engines make police cars
go fast.

Tough tires keep police cars rolling.

Police cars are easy to see. The light bar on top has red, white, blue, and amber lights.

Police cars are marked with the name of their community. How do they look in your town?

Police officers serve their community in many ways.   They often respond to **emergencies.**

Officers receive a call over a **two-way radio.** The call tells officers about a crime or an accident.

Officers rush to the scene. They use
the radio to speak with the station
house. The station house tells police
where help is needed.

Do you use a computer? Police cars have one right inside! Officers use the computer to find and store information.

A powerful **antenna** transmits signals to and from the radio.

Police officers drive around and watch for trouble. This is called **patrolling.**

Most police cars have a **radar** device. Officers use it to catch people driving too fast.

Officers can use radar inside or outside the police car.

Officers stop speeding drivers to give them a ticket.

A spotlight
helps officers
to spot trouble.

Police officers also find and catch
suspects. Suspects are people the
police believe have broken a law.

A suspect sits in the back seat of the police car. Heavy glass windows keep officers safe.

Police work can be dangerous. Each
car has a rifle in the front seat.
Officers can use the rifle to protect
themselves or others.

What do you think a **push bumper** does? It pushes cars and other things out of the way.

A police car's trunk holds special tools. Some are for first aid. Police officers use first-aid kits to help people who are hurt or sick.

Officers use their cars to work at special events. Police cars can block off roads.

This police car moves along with a
parade. The police are there to help in
case a problem comes up.

Police cars are powerful helpers. They help police officers keep us safe.

Fun Facts about Police Cars

■ Some police cars have a special compartment for a dog. Police dogs help officers with their work. Dogs use their powerful sense of smell to track and find suspects or missing people.

■ Police cars with dogs are called K-9 units. K-9 sounds like the word *canine,* which means like a dog.

■ The first police vehicles were pulled by horses.

■ Police radar works by sending out radio waves that bounce off a moving car. The waves return to the radar unit, which shows how fast the car is traveling.

Parts of a Police Car

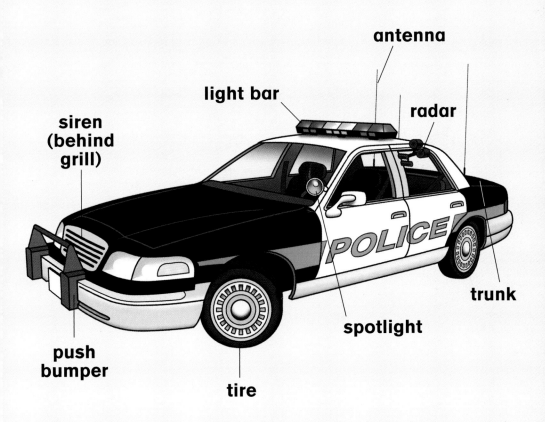

antenna

light bar

radar

siren
(behind
grill)

POLICE

trunk

push
bumper

spotlight

tire

29

Glossary

antenna: a rod that sends and receives two-way radio messages

emergencies: urgent needs for help

patrolling: moving around an area to keep it safe

push bumper: bars on a police car's front bumper that help move objects

radar: a device that sends out radio waves. Radio waves help find things like cars and can tell how fast they are going.

suspects: people believed to have broken a law

two-way radio: a device that sends and receives communication

Index

antenna, 14

computer, 13

engines, 6

light bar, 4, 8

push bumper, 23

radar, 16, 17

spotlight, 19

tires, 7

two-way radio, 11, 12

About the Author

Jill Braithwaite has worked with children's books for 11 years. She loves reading, writing, editing, and selling them. She also enjoys movies, walking, cooking, and playing with her pet ferret, Zaza. Jill lives in Minneapolis, Minnesota.

Photo Acknowledgments

The photographs in this book appear courtesy of: © Todd Strand/Independent Picture Service, front cover, pp. 6, 7, 9, 11, 13, 14, 15, 18, 19, 21, 22, 23, 24, 26, 31; © H. L. Stata/Image Finders, p. 3; © Royalty-Free/Corbis, p. 4; © Mikael Karlsson, pp. 5, 10, 16, 17, 25; © Jim Baron/Image Finders, pp. 8, 27; © T. Williams/The Image Finders, p. 12; © Novastock/Image Finders, p. 20.